The Toll Houses
of Norfolk

Patrick Taylor

POLYSTAR PRESS

ISBN 978 1 907154 02 7

The Toll-houses of Norfolk

Published by
Polystar Press
277 Cavendish Street
Ipswich Suffolk IP3 8BQ
(01473) 434604
polystar@ntlworld.com

ISBN 978 1 907154 02 7

Typeset by nattygrafix

Printed by
R Booth
The Praze, Penryn

Contents   Illustrations

for Reg Tricker

not a Norfolk boy

0.0 Introduction

As long ago as 1978, when I was fresh out of architectural school and living in Cornwall, it was resolved that toll-houses would be a worthwhile subject for further study - "one day" was the term used at the time I believe.

Years passed, life was got on with, and it was not until 1992 as a Cornishman abroad in Suffolk, that I went to study for an MA in Conservation Studies at the University of York. Here I encountered the phenomenon of local distinctiveness and realised that the toll-houses, built for the most part during the early industrial revolution before the coming of the railways, might be a good indicator. My dissertation in 1995 followed this hunch through and included as part of my study of local distinctiveness, a comparison between the toll-houses in the two counties I knew best, Cornwall and Suffolk. It would have included Norfolk too, had not the record office in Norwich burnt down in 1994, just as I started my research there.

Having published the results for Cornwall and drafted a volume for Suffolk, the time came to resume my studies of Norfolk and this book is the result. Like its companion volumes on Cornwall and Suffolk, it draws heavily on the original dissertation, together with new material specific to Norfolk, especially the gazetteer section.

My thanks must therefore go to my tutors at York and the staff at Norfolk Record Office and the Norwich Heritage Centre for their assistance with my research and illustrations. I must also thank Carol Haines of the Milestone Society, for making available her wealth of local knowledge and contacts, one of whom, Peter Allard, was particularly helpful with his encyclopaedic knowledge of Great Yarmouth.

Finally, the dedication which goes to my partner's father, for the help and support given by himself and his daughter whilst I have pursued this somewhat obscure study in a county close to his own.

Local Stone Toll-house,
Steanor Bottom, Littleborough,
Lancashire

1.0 The Turnpike Roads

Mending the Highways
(from Smith - 1970)

CAP. VIII.

The statute for mending of highways.

FOR amending of highways, being now both very noisom and tedious to travel in, and dangerous to all passengers and carriages :

(2) Be it enacted by the authority of this present parliament, that the constables and church-wardens of every parish within this realm, shall yearly upon the Tuesday or Wednesday in Easter week call together a number of the parishioners, and shall then elect and chuse two honest persons of the parish to be surveyors and orderers for one year, or the works for amendment of the highways in their parish leading to any market-town ; (3) the which persons shall have authority by virtue hereof, to order and direct the persons and carriages that shall be appointed for those works, by their discretions ; (4) and the said persons so named shall take upon them the execution of their said offices, upon pain every of them making default, to forfeit twenty shillings.

[margin: Who shall be charged towards the mending of highways. Surveyors shall be appointed for the amendment of highways. 3 Mod. 96. 22 Car.2.c.12. f. 12.]

II. And the said constables and church-wardens shall then also name and appoint four days for the amending of the said ways, before the feast of the nativity of Saint John Baptist then next following ; (2) and shall openly in the church the next Sunday after Easter give knowledge of the same four days ; (3) and upon the said days the parishioners shall endeavour themselves to the amending of the said ways ; (4) and shall be chargeable thereunto as followeth ; that is to say, every person for every plow-land in tillage or pasture that he or she shall occupy in the same parish, and every other person keeping there a draught or plough, shall find and send at every day and place to be appointed for the amending of the ways in that parish as is aforesaid, one wain or cart furnished after the custom of the country with oxen, horses or other cattle, and all other necessaries meet to carry things convenient for that purpose, and also two able men with the same, upon pain of every draught making default, ten shillings ; (5) and every other housholder, and also every cottager and labourer of that parish, able to labour, and being no hired servant by the year, shall by themselves or one sufficient labourer for every of them, upon every of the said four days, work and travel in the amendment of the said highways, upon pain of every person making default, to lose for every day twelve pence. (6) And if the said carriages of the parish, or any of them, shall not be thought needful by the supervisors to be occupied upon any of the said days, that then every such person that should have sent any such carriage, shall send to the said work for every carriage so spared two able men, there to labour for that day, upon pain to lose for every man so sent to the said work, twelve pence. (7) And every person and carriage abovesaid shall have and bring with them such shovels, spades, picks, mattocks,

[margin: Four days shall be appointed for the amendment of highways. Six days are appointed by 5 El. c.13. f.7. Each person's charge towards mending of highways. Explained by 18 El. c. 10; f. 2. Necessary tools shall be brought to be]

Statute for Mending of Highways, 1555
(from Serjeant & Penrose - 1973)

3

1.1 The King's Highway

In order to understand the turnpike road system that gave rise to toll-houses in the eighteenth century we need first to look at its origins in the mists of medieval time.

Early roads were not actual parcels of real estate set aside for the purpose of transit as have evolved today, but rather lines of least resistance where a 'right of passage' existed - the King's Highway - over ground that remained in private ownership. This still exists in vestigial form in our modern footpath network, which then as now consisted of three levels of usage: footpaths, bridleways and carriageways (now roads used as public paths). In those days diversions were implemented to maintain the right of the traveller if the road was 'founderous' or his way was blocked, rather than at the request of the owner to suit the management of the land as is now often the case.

The highway was thus a 'communal property right' available freely for the use of any subject of the Crown and as such received little or no maintenance other than out of selfish necessity to overcome a particular obstacle such as a flood or fallen tree. It was therefore in no individual's interest to invest time or money in repairing something that would mainly benefit others.

As a consequence the roads were generally in a very poor state and greatly abused by heavy loads with many horses, by spiked or narrow wheels and by the dragging of sledges or timber. Similar problems exist to this day where the selfish interest of highway users will require legislation to achieve a benefit for the common good (e.g. the limitation of motor car use), and it was indeed legislation then that was a first step on the way to improvement of the situation. A parallel can be seen here with another communal property right, that of the old strip field system with attendant grazing and hunting rights, which was also abused by selfish interest and eventually put to rights by the legislation of the Enclosure Acts.

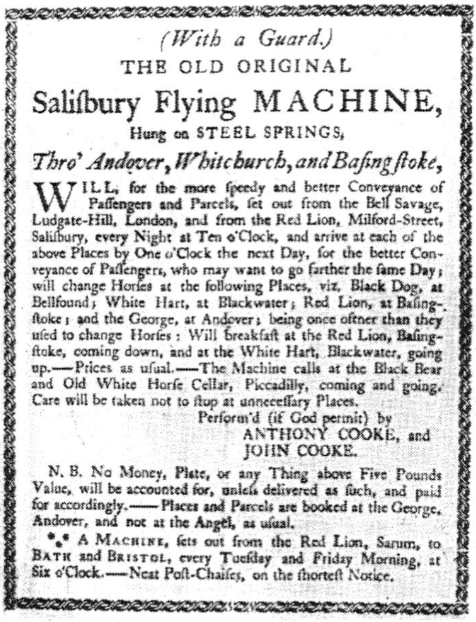

(With a Guard.)
THE OLD ORIGINAL
Salifbury Flying MACHINE,
Hung on STEEL SPRINGS,
Thro' Andover, Whitchurch, and Bafing ftoke,

WILL, for the more fpeedy and better Conveyance of Paffengers and Parcels, fet out from the Bell Savage, Ludgate-Hill, London, and from the Red Lion, Milford-Street, Salifbury, every Night at Ten o'Clock, and arrive at each of the above Places by One o'Clock the next Day, for the better Conveyance of Paffengers, who may want to go farther the fame Day; will change Horfes at the following Places, viz. Black Dog, at Bellfound; White Hart, at Blackwater; Red Lion, at Bafing-ftoke; and the George, at Andover; being once oftener than they ufed to change Horfes: Will breakfaft at the Red Lion, Bafing-ftoke, coming down, and at the White Hart, Blackwater, going up.——Prices as ufual.——The Machine calls at the Black Bear and Old White Horfe Cellar, Piccadilly, coming and going. Care will be taken not to ftop at unneceffary Places.

Perform'd (if God permit) by
ANTHONY COOKE, and
JOHN COOKE.

N. B. No Money, Plate, or any Thing above Five Pounds Value, will be accounted for, unlefs delivered as fuch, and paid for accordingly.——Places and Parcels are booked at the George, Andover, and not at the Angel, as ufual.

*** A MACHINE, fets out from the Red Lion, Sarum, to BATH and BRISTOL, every Tuefday and Friday Morning, at Six o'Clock.——Neat Poft-Chaifes, on the fhorteft Notice.

Salisbury Coach Service Poster
(from Wright - 1992)

1.2 Parish Responsibility

In the mid sixteenth century the state of the roads became of such concern that legislation was passed to firmly place the responsibility for their repair in the hands of the parish in which they were situated. The initial Act of 1555, in the brief reign of Mary Tudor, was a temporary measure which required each parish to elect two Surveyors. Their duty was to oversee the repair of roads by the inhabitants of that parish on four days per year when they were to provide 'statute labour'.

The larger landowners were also required to provide two men plus carts and tools whilst the Surveyors were permitted to dig for gravel on any waste land or commons adjoining the road. A further Act of 1562 extended the statute duties to six days per year and defaulters were liable to heavy fines.

Parishes that failed to maintain their roads properly were liable to be presented by the Justices to Quarter Sessions. If they then still failed to repair the roads satisfactorily they would be subject to indictment and the imposition of fines and/or additional days of statute labour. An occasional alternative to this was the raising of a Highway Rate by the Justices, which would then be used to pay for the necessary labour.

The problem which this system failed to tackle was that of the polluter not paying - the major users of the roads in a parish were not the inhabitants, but rather those passing through often with heavy loads for markets in other places. Their contribution to the effort of repair was made in their own parish and was but a fraction in recompense for the wear and tear they inflicted on the roads in general. The problem of selfish interest therefore remained during a period of increasing trade in the seventeenth century and was not helped by the unwillingness of labourers (one volunteer being worth ten pressed men) nor by Surveyors whose unpaid posts were held on an annual basis and led to low levels of skill and little continuity of effort.

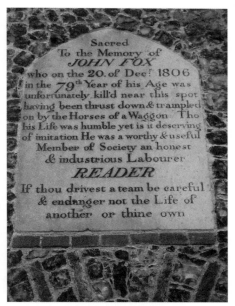

Death on the Roads: Memorial, Colney Church, Norfolk
photo: polystar

1.3 Available Technology

At the end of the seventeenth century in archaeological terms, the Iron Age was still very much in progress with timber, fired clay, stone and metal being the major materials for any significant undertaking. Power was sourced from either muscle, wind or water, all three being used in the various forms of mills at fixed locations, the former two for locomotion on land or water. The wonders of steam that could turn heat into motion were as yet unheard of and the nation's wealth was traded and defended by sailing ships of timber, tar and hemp rope.

The transportation of goods thus involved considerable effort and consequently costs away from the cheapest place of production rose sharply. A number of rivers had been made navigable but significant areas remained beyond the reach of water-borne transport. The roads thus acted as both feeders to the river system and as the main means of transport where the rivers did not reach. In addition some goods did not travel well by water, others might not risk military intervention at sea whilst even more were better walking themselves to market. Whilst road transport was many times more expensive per ton per mile, the differential being relatively less for more expensive goods, it was often the preferred alternative.

There was a large network of 'carriers' operating around the country, usually based at various inns and for the most part employing packhorses. The seventeenth century saw these augmented by increasing amounts of wheeled transport, largely as a result of the increasing size and quantity of goods being traded, which led ultimately to a renewed crisis on the roads. A response to this were the various 'Wheel Acts' which sought to limit the damage to the roads by legislating about permissible loads and wheel widths. These were doomed to failure as essentially against the spirit of the times they tried to contain the damage with preventative measures.

And whereas the Wheels of many Carts, Carrs, and Brewers Drays, now commonly used for the Carriage of Goods, Beer, Ale, and other things, from Place to Place within the Cities of London and Westminster, and Parishes aforesaid, where the Streets are Paved, are made thinner or narrower in the Felleys then formerly, and many are Shod with Iron Tyres, by means whereof the Pavements in the Streets of the said Cities and Places are daily impaired and broken up, and made dirty and rough: For prevention whereof for the time to come, Be it therefore Enacted by the Authority aforesaid, That from and after the Fifteenth day of December, the Wheels of every Cart, Carr or Dray to be used for the Carriage of any thing whatsoever, from any Place within the said Cities and Places, to any Place situate in the said Cities and Places where the Streets are Paved, shall be made to contain the full breadth of Six Inches in the Felley, and shall not be wrought about with any Iron Work whatsoever, nor be drawn with above the number of two Horses, after they are up the hills from the Water-side; And the Owners and Pro-

Extract from London Wheel Act, 1690
(from Searle - 1930)

1.4 Justice Trusts

The parish repair system had taken each parish's previous Common Law obligation to maintain local roads and enshrined it in national legislation which was not in fact abolished until the General Highway Act of 1835. The system contained no requirement for the improvement of roads to cater for increased usage and was essentially an evenly applied remedy to a very uneven problem. Considerable differences existed between parishes both in terms of size and the numbers of roads to repair, population density and availability of labour and local geology which affected both the quality of substrate and availability of materials for repair. A further overlay of differing amounts of road usage near towns as trade increased and carriers turned to waggons and coaches led to a result that included many extremes.

In some parishes the roads were doubtless adequate whilst in others they were difficult to start with, poorly repaired and subject to increasingly heavy usage. This final straw was the key to a solution, the earliest tolls levied to pay for repair being those charged by the Justice trusts of the late seventeenth century. The first of these dates from 1663 and was set up to remedy problems on part of the Great North Road, where the Justices had previously tried all else at their disposal without success.

The concept of tolls was not new and had in the past been used to fund both 'pavage' and 'pontage' as well as to recoup costs for occasional private roads. Tolls had also been levied for markets, giving rise to a different type of toll-house in medieval times. It was therefore no great leap to apply such a toll to remedy a problem on a particular public road, the Justices retaining control of both the tolled road and the others within a parish.

A further twelve Justice trusts were set up on particularly bad roads between 1696 and 1714 by which time the turnpike trust proper was beginning to emerge as a more suitable vehicle for setting the roads to rights.

15th Century Toll Bridge,
Mayton, Norfolk
photo: polystar

1.5 Turnpike Trusts

The earliest turnpike trusts date from 1707 and, although still under the control of the Justices who were usually included amongst their number anyway, were run by trustees who were able to spread the administrative load of managing the roads which was threatening to swamp the Justices' other duties. The trusts were composed for the most part of local gentlemen and landowners, who as trustees were not able to profit from the trust itself. They could however foresee the relief afforded to their parishes by the indirect benefits of improved local economies that would ensue from making outsiders pay for the maintenance of the local roads.

Turnpike trusts were but one of many types of local 'ad hoc' body set up during the eighteenth century amongst which are included the Incorporated Guardians of the Poor. These latter set up 'Unions' of several parishes to build a workhouse, which could then be let as a going concern to a local manufacturer who would feed the occupants in return for the use of their labour, thus relieving the parishes of the burden of the poor. These were as much forerunners of local authority Social Services departments as the turnpike trusts were of Highways departments, both marking the beginnings of bringing various systems into public control, without incurring great expense.

It should be remembered that the turnpike trusts were no more than non profit making trusts set up to manage existing routes, very unlike the later canal and railway concerns which were joint stock companies with shareholders whose aim was to create new routes and make money. Each turnpike trust was set up by an Act of Parliament, usually following vigorous petitioning by local worthies about the state of the roads. Parliamentary permission was necessary because the enterprise required the extinction of the former communal right of free passage and it became usual for Acts to last for a period of twenty one years, although renewal was usually forthcoming.

Anno X V.

Caroli II. Regis.

An Act for Repairing
the High-ways within the Counties of *Hertford*, *Cambridge* and *Huntington*.

 Whereas the ancient high-way and Post-Road leading from London to York, and so into Scotland, and like-wise from London into Lincolnshire, lieth for many miles in the Counties of Hertford, Cambridge and Huntington, in many of which places the Road, by reason of the great and many Loads which are weekly drawn in Waggons throughthe said places, as well by reason of the great Trade of Barley and Mault that cometh

Extract from First Turnpike Act, 1663
(from Searle - 1930)

1.6 Turnpike Mania

In the years up to 1750 some 133 turnpike trusts received their Acts of Parliament and roads were turnpiked in two main areas. Firstly, and mainly before 1720, the network of radial roads emanating from London were covered by a number of linear trusts, each one's territory abutting the next.

This process continued in the following thirty years alongside the second concentration of town-centred trusts which developed along the Severn valley between Bristol (at that time England's second largest city) and a rapidly developing Birmingham. Around mid-century the turnpike idea seems to have captured the imagination in a big way and between 1751 and 1772 a further 418 Acts were passed, which effectively allowed the turnpike system to cover the country.

The uncertainties that led up to the American War of Independence brought this age of confidence to a sudden halt in 1773 and the ensuing years that also included the Napoleonic Wars saw greatly reduced activity in terms of new trusts. A further 400 or so trusts were set up between 1773 and 1836 of which 59 alone were in the years 1824 to 1826.

These later years of lesser activity were due in part to a saturation point being reached but should also be seen against the beginnings of the years of the boom in canal building from 1770 along with the industrial revolution getting into full swing, doubtless helped along its way by the greatly improved transport, trade and communications links provided by the turnpikes. The final mini-boom in turnpike activity of 1824 to 1826, probably represents a mopping up of the last remaining suitable routes in slightly improved times. Whilst Acts continued to be renewed throughout most of the nineteenth century, the last new Act of 1836 foreshadows the coming of the railways in the 1840's and the growing realisation that the days of the turnpikes were numbered.

Toll-house Door, Wiggenhall
(*Wisbech - South Lynn etc*)
photo: polystar

MELTON.

MESSRS. LENNY AND SMITH

Are honored with instructions from the Trustees of the Ipswich and Southtown Turnpike, to Sell by Auction,

AT THE COACH AND HORSES INN, MELTON,

ON

Monday next, October 28th, 1872

AT TWO O'CLOCK PRECISELY,

The undermentioned Valuable Properties, in Lots under such Conditions as will then and there be produced.

NAMELY. LOT I.--The substantially erected

FREEHOLD BUILDING CALLED MELTON

TOLL HOUSE

with Shed for water carts & tools, & a large piece of excellent garden ground having a frontage upon the Main Road of about 160 feet, & another upon the Asylum Road of about 126 feet; also the toll gate & posts. LOT 2.—The materials of the Toll House at Rushmere, with the gate & posts. LOT 3.—The side gate & posts with Keepers' Hut at Kesgrave. LOT 4.—Water Cart. LOT 5.—Ditto. LOT 6.—Ditto. LOT 7.—Snow plough. LOT 8.—Wheelbarrow. LOT 9.—Ditto. LOT 10.—Ditto. LOT 11.—Ditto. LOT 12.—Pick and three stone hammers. LOT 13.—Ditto. LOT 14.—Brush bill, adze and hoe. LOT 15.—Ditto. LOT 16.—Rake and sieve. LOT 17.—Three hoes and three hammers. Also if not previously disposed of by private contract. LOT 18.—An iron pump on Rushmere Heath. LOT 19.—Ditto at Playford. LOT 20.—Two iron pumps at Kesgrave. LOT 21.—An Iron Pump at Martlesham. LOT 22.—An Iron Pump at Woodbridge. LOT 23.—Ditto at Woodbridge (near the nursery). LOT 24.—An iron pump at Melton. LOT 25.—Ditto at Melton, (next the Parish Land). LOT 26.—Ditto at Melton, (next the property of JAMES PACKE ESQ.) LOT 27.—An iron pump at Ufford. LOT 28.—Ditto at Petistree. LOT 29.—Ditto against the County Bridge at Wickham Market.

Further information may be obtained of R. B. Baas, Esq., Solicitor, and of the Auctioneers, Halesworth.

S. B. FYFE, PRINTER, HALESWORTH.

Toll-house Sale Poster, 1872
(from Serjeant & Penrose - 1973)

10

1.7 Winding Up

By the 1840's the turnpike road system had reached its greatest extent with over 20,000 miles of road under the control of over a thousand trusts. During the preceding century the growth and improvement of the system had greatly reduced travelling times and consequently enlarged the market place. Road construction techniques had gradually improved from the early days of simply piling another layer of gravel on top to the latter years, under the influence of great engineers like Telford or McAdam, when roads were rebuilt with a firm foundation and progressively smaller sized stones rolled in, to provide a freely draining cambered finish.

Inland transportation as a whole, with the complementary system of canals, had been greatly improved but not revolutionised, as it was still essentially bound by the limitations of muscle and wind power. It was the magic of steam in the form of the railways which ultimately brought the revolution. The turnpike system suffered first followed by the canals, as both were swept away as passengers and then freight took to the rails.

The turnpike trusts were thus subjected to falling receipts through the mid-nineteenth century which made it increasingly difficult for them to deliver the goods.

Lack of repairs led to a growing resentment to their charges amongst their customers, perhaps most strongly felt in Wales where the 'Rebecca' Riots of the 1840's saw the destruction of many gates and toll-houses by men disguised in female clothing, in imitation of the biblical Rebecca and her daughters.

By the 1870's the trusts were being wound up, their assets in the form of toll-houses and equipment were sold off, and the responsibility for the roads, which they still did not own, vested in the Highway Boards, forerunners of the County Councils.

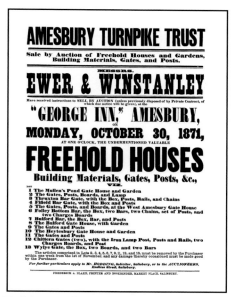

Toll-house Sale Poster, 1871
(from Wright - 1992)

2.0 Collecting the Tolls

Toll Gate Collection
(from Smith - 1970)

A TABLE of the TOLLS payable at this TURNPIKE GATE.
[By the Local Act.]

	s	d
FOR every Horse, Mule, Afs, or other Beast (Except Dogs) drawing any Coach, Berlin, Landau, Barouche, Chariot, Chaise, Chair, Hearse, Gig, Curricle, Whiskey, Taxed Cart, Waggon, Wain, Timber frame, Cart frame, Dray or other Vehicle of whatsoever description when drawn by more than one Horse or other Beast the Sum of Four pence half-penny Such Waggon, Wain, Cart, or other such Carriage having Wheels of lefs breadth than four and a half inches _____		4½
AND when drawn by one Horse or other Beast only the sum of six pence (Waggons, Wains and other such Carriages having Wheels as aforesaid)	"	6
FOR every Dog drawing any Truck, Barrow or other Carriage for the space of One Hundred Yards or upwards upon any part of the said Roads, the Sum of One Penny _____	"	1
FOR every Horse, Mule, Afs, or other Beast laden or unladen and not drawing, the Sum of Two-pence _____	"	2
FOR every carriage moved or propelled by Steam or Machinery or by any other power than Animal power the Sum of one Shilling for each Wheel thereof _____	1	0
FOR every Score of Oxen, Cows or neat Cattle, the Sum of Ten-pence and so in Proportion for any greater or lefs Number _____	"	10
FOR every Score of Calves, Sheep, Lambs or Swine the Sum of Five pence and so in proportion for any greater or lefs Number _____	"	5

(By 4. G. 4. C. 95)

	s	d
FOR every Horse, Mule, Afs or other Beast drawing any Waggon Wain, Cart or other such Carriage having the Fellies of the Wheels of the breadth of Six Inches or upwards at the Bottom when drawn by more than one Horse, Mule, Afs or other Beast the Sum of Three-pence		3
AND when drawn by one Horse, Mule, Afs or other Beast the Sum of Four-Pence (Except Carts) _____	"	4
FOR every Horse, Mule, Afs or other Beast drawing any Waggon Wain, Cart or other such Carriage having the Fellies of the Wheels of the Breadth of four inches and a half and lefs than Six inches when drawn by more than one Horse, Mule, Afs or other Beast the Sum of Three-pence three farthings _____		3¾
AND when drawn by one Horse, Mule, Afs or other Beast the Sum of Five-pence (Except Carts) _____	"	5
FOR every Horse, Mule, Afs or other Beast drawing any Cart with Wheels of every Breadth when drawn by only one such Animal the Sum of Six Pence _____	"	6

NB Two Oxen or neat Cattle drawing shall be considered as one Horse

3. G. 4. C. 126.

CARRIAGES with four Wheels affixed to any Waggon or Cart all as if drawn by two Horses. Carriages with two Wheels so d pay Toll as if drawn by one Horse but such Carriages are Tolls if conveying any Goods other than for Protection.

Toll Board from Sussex
(from Harris - no date)

2.1 Toll Gates & Turnpikes

The turnpike trusts were generally empowered by their Acts of Parliament to 'erect or cause to be erected a gate or gates, turnpike or turnpikes', usually in positions that were left to their own discretion. Certain towns did lobby Parliament and as a result toll-gates could not be placed nearer than three miles distant so as not to discourage local markets. Trusts with linear routes therefore tended to have toll-gates at either end of their territory with occasional others inbetween, often where a side road joined the way. In contrast the town-centred trusts tended to end up with a ring of toll gates around the outskirts guarding virtually every road inwards.

The trusts were however compelled to enforce a strictly defined set of toll charges that were to a large degree proportional to the amounts of damage caused by differing types of traffic. Local traffic was often favoured by being allowed a same day return trip at no extra cost and there were a number of common exemptions from toll, notably people going to church or to vote, agricultural traffic, the Army and mail coaches which sounded their horns on approaching the gates.

Most trusts had three main employees: a surveyor to initiate and oversee repairs together with a clerk and treasurer to administer their affairs. Their tasks were to engage labour as required to mend the roads and oversee the collectors employed at each toll-gate. There was an inherent weak link in the system here that depended on the honesty of the collectors or pike-men as they became known. This led in due course to the practice of toll-farming, whereby the proceeds of a toll-gate for the coming year were sold off by auction to 'toll-farmers', either individual collectors with initiative, or contractors who took on themselves the risk of employing several collectors. The trusts were thus assured of a toll income, which was often supplemented by composition payments from parishes who bought themselves out of their statutory labour obligations.

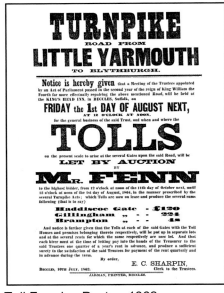

Toll Farming Poster, 1862
(from Serjeant & Penrose - 1973)

2.2 Toll-houses

To facilitate the twenty four hour presence of their collectors, the turnpike trusts usually built small associated dwellings at their gates:- the toll-houses. They generally comprised very minimal accommodation of two rooms with a scullery and privy attached, although larger types did become more common in later years. The larger ones were probably the result of toll-farming, the houses being bid for at auction both as generators of toll income and as accommodation for the pike-men. These toll-houses were either one or two storeyed and thus came in many shapes and sizes, some trusts adopting a standard design whilst others seem to have tried many variations.

If built to a normal rectangular plan they would often have gable windows very close to the front corner of the building or a bay window on the main room to provide the collector with a view up and down the road. A development of the bay came in the form of the octagonal ended house where effectively the bay became the room, this particular form becoming the norm for the toll-house building-type to such an extent that it was also employed at toll collection points on the canals. The octagonal shape also appears in some country house park gatekeeper's lodges, where again an element of control was required.

It may thus have its roots in the neo-classical love of geometry or possibly may be derived from military precedents of a defensive nature, as many toll-houses of the more ornate 'gothick' kind sport the mock battlements of the picturesque. Wherever the shape derived from, it was nevertheless of great utility.

Much can be said for the presence of the buildings themselves; their many windows and forward position would undoubtedly have unsettled any approaching traveller intent on avoiding the toll with a feeling of having his every move watched. It is this presence that remains today as such a helpful clue to identifying toll-houses, particularly when they are not of the obvious octagonal type.

Octagonal Gate-house, Felbrigg
photo: polystar

Whilst the pike-man's job required his presence on the premises it was not strictly necessary for him to be on guard looking out of the windows twenty four hours of the day. Most toll-houses were built on very small parcels of land owned by the trustees, usually carved out of the corners of fields, but sufficient to allow the tenants a small cottage garden for their home grown produce. Because of their usual remoteness these small plots often also contained their own well or pump for water supply.

Internally the toll-houses would have been very cramped by modern day standards, particularly if the pike-man had a family of any size. The small bedroom would have slept the whole family, a truckle bed for the children sliding out from beneath the main one, as can be seen at the Sussex toll-house at the Weald and Downland Museum. The other room served every other purpose, being in every sense the living room, and contained the hearth where food was cooked, together with seating, tables, storage etc. and may well have been awkward to furnish if without any square corners at all. The main door to the highway usually led off this room and it was often protected by a porch or shelter of some kind where the collector could receive tolls in the dry.

Another common indicative feature of toll-houses is a blank space where a toll-board would have been placed. This could be a filled in window at first floor or a space adjoining an asymmetrically placed door on the ground floor. Sited as they were hard against the highway, the toll-houses that survive today are perhaps the most visible remains of the turnpike system. The keen industrial archaeologist will also be able to find many examples of milestones, a later requirement of the legislation, still shown as 'MS' on modern Ordnance Survey maps. There are also a few surviving gates, their general form consisting of a main vehicular gate or turnpike (originally a spiked pole), with usually a pedestrian gate between this and the toll-house.

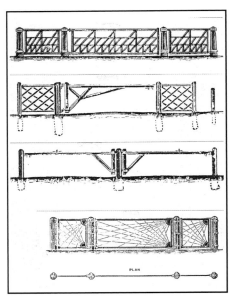

Varieties of Toll Gate
(from Searle - 1930)

16

2.3 Local Distinctiveness

A particular problem with toll-houses is dating their construction. In between a *terminus post quem* of the original turnpike act and a *terminus ante quem* of finding them on a tithe map or early Ordnance Survey lie many years. Most will be found to have been constructed nearer the earlier date at the beginning of a turnpike's existence and therefore not benefiting from the slightly improved communications that followed by overland transport. They were even less likely to have benefited from the greater improvements that the canals later brought to water borne transport, and certainly missed out on the radically changed face of building material distribution ushered in by the railway age.

In terms of their walling materials therefore, toll-houses were almost universally built of what was locally available and remain to this day useful pointers to local distinctiveness and the nature of the geology thereabouts. Thus in Plymouth we find the local Devonian limestone used, in Bath an Oolitic limestone, in Anglesey the local metamorphic rock and near Todmorden, in the Pennines, Millstone Grit (see p.1). As eighteenth century buildings, where stone was not available, brick was usually the order of the day, so that in Cambridge we find white Gault bricks, whilst in Essex red brick and tile from the London Clay.

Local Devonian Limestone Toll-house in Plymouth
(from Searle - 1930)

Although the timber-frame tradition had long gone into decline, and certainly was less suitable for forming an octagonal building, there is a timber-framed and thatched toll-house in Suffolk and the lap-boarded Sussex example in the Weald and Downland Museum, both of which are rectangular in plan.

Roofing materials show a similar pattern. Thatch was the material of an earlier age and unsuitable anyway as it required more frequent repair and maintenance, diverting the trust's funds away from the roads. It also represented a severe fire risk, especially in towns, a definite liability should there be any local dissent about the coming of the turnpikes. Pantiles and the larger stone flags and tiles were often the locally available preference. Whilst not best suited to the small areas of hipped roofs involved in octagonal buildings, they were sometimes used nevertheless, more so on the rectangular examples. Slate, however, was the new material of the age and seems to have been the predominant choice, even in the east where it had to be imported from afar. In the eighteenth century roofs were generally pitched according to the materials used, a slate or pantile roof requiring less timber at 30° to 40° pitch, than would a plaintile roof at 45° or more.

We have seen that toll-houses were basic small domestic buildings, housing persons fairly low down the social scale. As such they fit within the vernacular tradition, although the tendency has been for them to be studied as curiosities within the province of the industrial archaeologist. Within this vernacular tradition they may be considered somewhere near its later threshold, as particularly with the octagonal forms, there is an overlay of the 'polite', a signalling of their purpose as a particular type of building. This is especially true where a standard design marks their belonging to a particular trust or they venture into the 'picturesque' at the whim of the trustees. The fashionable input could manifest itself as 'gothick' windows or even crenellated parapets, which by this time presumably no longer required the King's licence.

These fashions were however directed from above, being very much the prerogative of the trustees, who as fashionable members of the gentry would have been very aware of the latest ideas and as keen to try them out on their turnpike roads as at their lodge gates. It is therefore possible that the octagonal form used in toll-houses derived from earlier garden buildings of this shape, as is believed to have happened with park lodge gatehouses. The turnpike roads can be seen in this light as a parallel phenomenon to the enclosures and creation of our country house estates. The gentry not only came to control large areas of land, signalling this benign stewardship with their various gatekeeper's lodges, but also the routes between the major centres, controlled by the toll-houses.

2.4 What Lies Ahead?

Local distinctiveness relates to the customs and ways of doing things that have evolved in an area, and which give it a distinctive local character. This 'difference from other places' appears not only in the landscape moulded by our management of the land but also in our built environment. An important part of maintaining local distinctiveness therefore involves celebrating the differences, keeping alive the stories and associations of a place.

The problem with toll-houses in this respect is their situation. They were mostly built in isolation, on the perimeters of our settlements and as a consequence almost never occur within our historic centres, where most modern day celebration of place happens. Whilst the turnpikes probably initiated ribbon development, encouraging the spread of suburban villas, their remains are now largely surrounded by it, so that apart from their intimate link with the actual road, toll-houses have little sense of place.

Unfortunately the road itself has become too fast and dangerous a place to encourage anyone to stop and wonder. Meanwhile our canals and railways, which move at a more human pace, have become the subjects of the majority of transport nostalgia, and thus leisure activity.

The major residual usage of toll-houses is as dwellings and as such they are cramped and therefore often extended; they are poorly serviced because of their remoteness and often unpleasantly sited on the highway edge. We therefore find our remaining toll-houses the unconsidered remnants of a forgotten system, infrequently listed unless tending towards the more 'polite' and severely at risk from future road developments.

In order to celebrate what is left, we need to take the first step in recognising it. Accordingly we will now look at Norfolk's turnpike roads and toll-houses in greater detail.

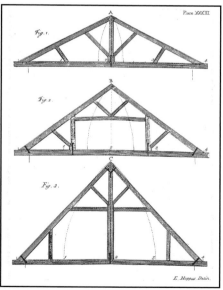

Varieties of Roof Pitch for
Different Roofing Materials
(from Cruickshank & Wyld - 1975)

19

3.0 The Norfolk Turnpikes

Stagecoach and Four
(from Smith - 1970)

photo: peter allard

Toll Board, Vauxhall, Great Yarmouth
(Great Yarmouth - Acle etc.)

photo: polystar

Toll Board Remains, Scoulton Gate
(Norwich - Watton)

3.1 Norfolk Turnpike Trusts

Norfolk was fairly typical of the country as a whole in terms of turnpike activity through the eighteenth and early nineteenth centuries, its roads spread throughout the period with a recognisable boom around 1770. Its first turnpike act was relatively early for the provinces and in 1695 dealt with a particularly bad section of the Norwich to London road, that between Wymondham and Attleborough. Norwich at that time was a prosperous cathedral city with a large agricultural hinterland which had encouraged its growth as a centre for trade.

Seventy years passed without further activity until in 1765 acts were passed for several roads in the Fens, two of which came into Norfolk from Wisbech, one to Downham Market the other to Kings Lynn. In the meantime the original London road turnpike had been extended in 1767 to link Norwich right through to Thetford on the Suffolk border. Further acts followed in the boom years of 1769 to 1772, one group of trusts making further connections around Kings Lynn and Downham Market, another group linking Norwich with Scole and New Buckenham to the south, Caister to the east, and Swaffham and Watton to the west.

A little after the boom, in 1785 the Ipswich to South Town turnpike had linked Great Yarmouth, via Lowestoft along what is now the A12 east coast road, and included a branch off serving Bungay. In 1796 the Little Yarmouth to Blythburgh turnpike provided an alternative route out of this southeast corner of the county via Beccles.

Eventually links were made northwards from Norwich, to Aylsham in 1794, North Walsham in 1797 and Fakenham and Wells in 1823 and 1826. Finally in 1830 Great Yarmouth was connected to the Norwich-Caister road by the Acle turnpike. Although none of these turnpikes were actually town-centred, at the end of the day both Kings Lynn and especially Norwich had become hubs for a number of linear trusts.

Milestone, Mattishall
(*Norwich - Swaffham etc.*)
photo: polystar

3.2 Chalk and Ice

Geologically Norfolk is for the most part underlain by chalk, the youngest and purest of limestones laid down in the Cretaceous period some 100 million years ago. It is however not the chalk of our high downlands, but rather of relatively low lying gently rolling countryside. Within the chalk, and left as a deposit in its surface layer of clay, are found numerous flints, the silica rich nodules that have crystallised out separately from the original calcareous ooze that settled to form the chalk.

In the far west of the county running north-south from Hunstanton past Kings Lynn and Downham Market, there is immediately underlying the chalk a thin belt of the Early Cretaceous Greensand and Gault clay exposed. Beyond this small escarpment lies the Wash where the even older Late Jurassic Kimmeridge clay beds have been largely removed by the action of ice and replaced by the recent peaty deposits of fenland.

In the east of the county, the chalk is buried beneath the more recent Norwich crag deposits, sands and clays of the late Pliocene period, laid down in estuarine conditions preceding the Ice Ages of the last million years or so.

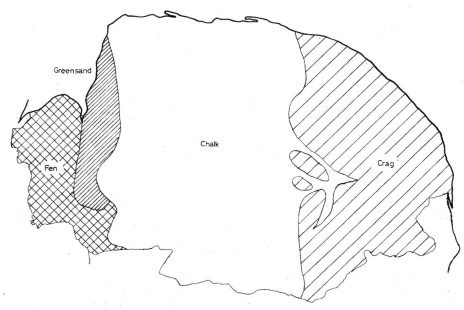

The Geology of Norfolk

3.3 Timber and Clay

In central and east Norfolk the chalk and crag deposits are covered by heavy glacial boulder clay soils, so good for the wheat production that makes East Anglia the granary of Britain. There is thus a contrast between the heavy clay soils of 'High Norfolk' and the lighter sandy soils of south-western Norfolk, known as Breckland, that have become heathland through the leaching of nutrients that followed man's deforestation.

Whilst Breckland was stripped of its trees fairly early on in man's history, the clay lands remained wooded to some extent right through to medieval times. This is largely due to the retention of woodland areas, managed on a cycle of coppicing to produce regular supplies of underwood and timber. However, by the sixteenth century with the period of timber frame construction at its peak, a shortage of timber meant that this Norfolk 'vernacular' only preserved a local tradition in building, much of its materials being imported from the Baltic. The underwood was still used for wattle and daub infill and the chalk of central Norfolk provided the raw material for a busy lime-burning industry. The local form that evolved was not one of exposed timber framing as seen in the west of England, but rather the more subtle use of lime renders and washes, the timber only appearing externally in jetties and exposed corner posts.

The presence of suitable clays meant that Norfolk figures relatively early in the rise of the popularity of brick. This was used occasionally to infill timber framing but really came into its own in the seventeenth and eighteenth centuries when many a timber-framed building was given a brick front, typically with a steep plaintiled roof tucked behind a parapet giving away the true construction. The bricks came in two main varieties, red or white, the former a very soft sandy brick, easily rubbed, the latter a harder buff coloured brick, both of which were often used together, one providing the detailed work to the other's use en masse.

Because Norfolk's chalk is geologically mainly from the upper strata, it was not very suitable for use on its own as clunch, however along with flint, pebbles and cobbles, especially in the north of the county, it was often used as a facing material usually combined with red brick quoins and dressings. Similarly there was a substantial use of Carstone from the greensand beds in the west of the county, usually with white brick dressings. These materials come lower down the social scale as does the use of the heavy boulder clay in the far south of the county bordering Suffolk for clay lump construction, a form of prefabricated cob.

3.4 Norfolk Toll-houses

Norfolk's first toll-houses were probably those of the Wymondham to Attleborough road, later extended to take in Norwich and Thetford at its ends, but unfortunately nothing remains to confirm this.

The two early fenland trusts of 1765 have left us a collection of 'Telford' type toll-houses south-west of Kings Lynn. Brick built bungalows with a central octagonal bay and originally slate roofs, of a design used by the great engineer on many of his Scottish roads. They probably date from around 1820, when he was heavily involved with the drainage of the fens and constructing the road across the Wash. This design was however not adopted elsewhere in Norfolk, nor was the octagonal toll-house used as found so commonly elsewhere in Britain.

The large number of trusts set up in the boom around 1770 adopted designs not unlike those adopted at this time further south in Suffolk. The Norwich to Swaffham trust used both one and two storey rectangular toll-houses with simple gabled roofs in pantiles. The large two storey toll-houses at Earlham and East Tuddenham would not be out of place in central Suffolk, nor would the single storey one at Etling Green be out of place in eastern Suffolk.

This single storey rectangular brick construction with a gabled pantile roof seems to have been the norm adopted by the later Norfolk trusts in the east of the county, presumably for the same reasons as it was adopted in Suffolk. The timber frame tradition was essentially one of rectangular buildings, and with pantiles the local preference for roofs, the difficulties of constructing octagonal hips would have been avoided.

Good examples of these can be found on the 1794 Cromer road at Marsham, the 1796 Little Yarmouth road at Haddiscoe and the 1797 North Walsham road at Stone Cross.

Window detail, Salters Lode
(*Wisbech - Downham Market*)
photo: polystar

Whilst the turnpike roads of western Norfolk eventually complemented and allowed the crossing of the rivers and ditches of the Fens, those in eastern Norfolk seem to have avoided the navigable areas of the Broads, only the Great Yarmouth road venturing eastwards from Norwich. This may be due to the extension of the river system there by canalisation: the Aylsham Navigation of 1779, the North Walsham and Dilham Canal of 1826 along with the 'Navigations' of the Yare and Waveney that improved water borne access to Norwich and Bungay respectively.

The later Norfolk turnpike trusts in the final boom years of the 1820's seem to have favoured the hipped roof in slate in place of the gabled pantile. The 1823 Norwich to Fakenham trust's toll-house at Bawdeswell is unusually hipped pantile, whilst the 1826 Wells to Fakenham trust's two surviving toll-houses at Wells and Walsingham are both brick with hipped slate roofs.

The final Norfolk trust connecting Norwich to Great Yarmouth via the Acle Straight in 1830 has left no surviving toll-houses, but we do know that the Vauxhall toll-house of 1852 was octagonal, of brick and slate, probably the only one such in Norfolk, and of such a late date adjoining a railway station, likely to be of imported materials.

Perhaps the most striking thing that emerges about Norfolk's toll-houses is that they do not seem to follow any particular pattern, no two that remain are the same, even within the same turnpike trust. In addition there is a decided scarcity of what might be considered the 'normal' octagonal form more prevalent elsewhere in the country.

As a result of this, after the following gazetteer section describing the county's toll-houses, there will be found an appendix illustrating other octagonal buildings around the county - they do exist, it is just that they are not toll-houses.

Side Window Detail, Marsham
(*Norwich - Aylsham etc.*)
photo: polystar

4.0 A Norfolk Gazetteer

The remainder of this book comprises a gazetteer of both toll-houses and their former sites. In general all surviving toll-houses are illustrated and given a map reference without brackets. Those that have been lost, but where a suitable photograph has been forthcoming, are also illustrated but given bracketed references. The remaining toll-house sites, lost completely without trace other than documentary, are described as far as possible in the boxes at the foot of each page. Those that appeared as 'T.G.' or 'T.P.' on the first edition Ordnance Survey maps of c.1838 are so marked.

The gazetteer starts in the far north-west of the county, with the toll-houses around King's Lynn, then runs anticlockwise around Norwich, concluding with links to the south-east and Great Yarmouth. Purists may question the validity of including a few from just into Cambridgeshire or over the Ouse or Waveney, but they are there for completeness; no county stands alone.

The author is very conscious of this being a first attempt to document these buildings in such detail and would be very grateful to hear of any errors, omissions, additional information or photographic evidence in respect of any toll-house that readers might be aware of.

Readers should be aware that most of our surviving toll-houses are now in private ownership as people's homes, please respect this. The author apologises in advance to any owners for any nuisance this publication might bring their way, and hopes the benefits of wider knowledge of this obscure subject can be seen to outweigh any inconvenience caused.

It is certainly hoped that a good many owners will come to appreciate their guardianship of this small part of our heritage, and perhaps a few more of these unique buildings will in due course get the added protection of becoming listed buildings, rather than become the subjects of memorials like the adjoining illustration.

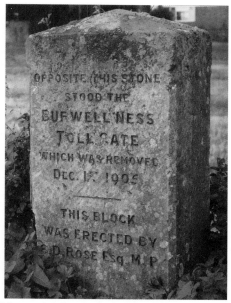

Memorial Stone for Burwell Ness
Toll-house, Cambridgeshire
photo: polystar

Date	Act	Turnpike
1695	7/8 WIII c.26	Norwich, Wymondham - Attleborough etc.
1765	5 GIII c.82	Chatteris Ferry, Wisbech - Downham Market
1765	5 GIII c.101	Wisbech - South Lynn etc.
1769	9 GIII c.66	Norwich - Scole Bridge
1769	9 GIII c.68	Norwich - Caister Causeway
1770	10 GIII c.54	Norwich - Block Hill
1770	10 GIII c.67	Norwich - Swaffham etc.
1770	10 GIII c.77	Norwich - Watton
1770	10 GIII c.78	Stoke Ferry - Barton etc.
1770	10 GIII c.85	Kings Lynn - Stoke Ferry etc.
1770	10 GIII c.86	Kings Lynn - Hillington etc.
1770	10 GIII c.97	Littleport - Downham Market
1772	12 GIII c.95	Norwich - New Buckenham
1772	12 GIII c.98	Downham Market - Barton etc.
1794	34 GIII c.114	Norwich - Aylsham etc.
1796	36 GIII c.142	Little Yarmouth - Blythburgh
1797	37 GIII c.147	Norwich - North Walsham
1823	4 GIV c.80	Norwich - Fakenham
1826	7 GIV c.136	Wells - Fakenham etc.
1830	11 GIV c.39	Great Yarmouth - Acle etc.

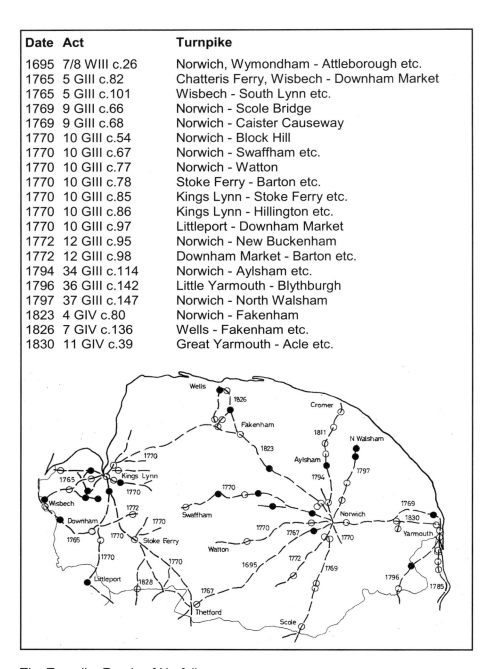

The Turnpike Roads of Norfolk

Clenchwarton Toll-house
TF 579203   'T.P.'
Wisbech - South Lynn etc.

photo: polystar

This small bungalow just west of Kings Lynn controlled the old road into Lincolnshire north-westwards across the Wash. It has a small central octagonal bay with a doorway and two windows, although this is now less apparent with the roof having been remodelled.

This is known as a 'Telford' type toll-house, more typical of the west and north of Britain where this engineer worked on many turnpike trusts. This type seems to have been popular in this area of fenland as we shall see in the following pages.

As indicated above it appeared on the first edition 1" Ordnance Survey maps as 'T.P.'

Cross Keys Toll-house
(TF 509199)   'T.P.'
Wisbech - South Lynn etc.

The turnpike road north-westwards from Kings Lynn had a second toll-house within Norfolk at Walpole Cross Keys. From here the road continued across the county border into Lincolnshire, and then across the River Nene to where there was a further toll-house at Sutton Bridge.

The Walpole St Andrew tithe apportionment of 1840 lists the building as 'Toll Bar House and Garden' owned by 'Turnpike Trustees'.

Thornton's Bridge Toll-house
TF 574139   'T.P.'
Wisbech - South Lynn etc.

Strategically placed at the top of a T-junction, this toll-house controlled the road over Thornton's Bridge in the parish of Tilney cum Islington, four miles south-west of Kings Lynn.

Another 'Telford' type toll-house, this one at least retains the roof shape over the bay. It has however been retiled in modern concrete roof tiles, and is also now rendered. Presumably it originally had facing brickwork and a slate roof like the fine example at Wiggenhall shown opposite.

Islington Lodge Toll-house
(TF 582172)   'T.P.'
Wisbech - South Lynn etc.

Although the Clenchwarton tithe records make no mention of Turnpike Trusts, the map shows the Clenchwarton toll-house and the apportionment includes a second site, privately owned but described as 'Toll Bar House'.

The map shows a building on a small plot adjoining the road, three miles out of Kings Lynn on the main Wisbech road near Islington Lodge. This would certainly be an ideal site for a toll-house, but nothing now remains.

Wiggenhall St Mary Toll-house
TF 596117   'T.P.'
Wisbech - South Lynn etc.

photo: polystar

On the west bank of the River Great Ouse five miles south of Kings Lynn, the parish of Wiggenhall St Mary Magdalen boasts a further 'Telford' type toll-house. This one is in much nearer its original condition, perhaps the best preserved in Norfolk and listed grade II.

The brickwork here has only been painted and it retains its slate roof with lead-rolled hips. Best of all, though are the 'gothick' style windows and pointed arch doorway, so typical of this era.

Wiggenhall South Toll Gate
(TF 597113)   'Toll'
Wisbech - South Lynn etc.

About a quarter mile south of the toll-house illustrated above, the old 1" Ordnance Survey maps show 'Toll' at a T-junction, from where one road heads off eastwards across the River Great Ouse towards the village of Watlington.

As nothing remains now, and the other toll-house was so near, it is unclear whether this was the site of a further toll-house, or possibly just a side gate.

Lords Bridge Toll-house
TF 571123   'T.P.'
Wisbech - South Lynn etc.

photo: polystar

About a mile south of Thornton's Bridge another bridge crosses the same drain, the Smeeth Lode Mill Basin.

Here we can find a toll-house of a different type, fairly common across the rest of west and central Norfolk.The Lords Bridge toll-house is a two storey hipped roof house, which has presumably had some of its openings, including the main road door, blocked up.

Its position tight on the corner of two roads that cross would give the necessary presence and feel of control needed by a toll-house.

Walpole Highway Toll-house
(TF 525143)   'T.P.'
Wisbech - South Lynn etc.

Three miles west of Thornton's Bridge, at Walpole Highway there was a further toll-house, now gone like the Islington Lodge one, which it might have replaced.

Roughly mid-way between Kings Lynn and Wisbech it controlled what is now a minor road, which was until very recently the main A47.

Lynn Road Toll-house, Wisbech (Cambs)
TF 467104   'T.P.'
Wisbech - South Lynn etc.

photo: polystar

The Wisbech to South Lynn turnpike road was part of a much larger trust covering much of the north Cambridgeshire fens.

The 'Lynn Road' from Wisbech towards Kings Lynn was controlled by this toll-house about half a mile outside Norfolk, north-east of the town centre, near Walsoken.

The building is of three bays with a central doorway fronting the main road with a blanked out window over for the toll-board. It is built of local dark bricks and now has a replacement concrete tile roof.

Downham Road Toll-house
(TF 466090)   'T.P.'   **(Cambs)**
Wisbech - Downham Market

The 'Downham Road' from Wisbech also had its toll-house, again about half a mile outside Norfolk, this time south-east of the town centre towards Emneth.

This one has now gone, probably as a result of the dual carriageway now approaching the town along this route. Wisbech originally had seven toll-houses, guarding the various approaches to the town, most now demolished.

Outwell Toll-house
TF 535028
Wisbech - Downham Market

photo: polystar

East of the village of Outwell, indeed further east than early OS maps show ('T.P.' at TF 520037) this small bungalow goes by the name of 'Tolbar'. It sits hard on the highway edge at a road junction and certainly looks the part.

The current owner confirmed that there was at one time a small gable window on the eastern side, now widened into an internal doorway through to the extension.

Unfortunately the tithe map for Outwell has proved elusive, so that a moved site to suit local needs can only be guessed at.

Suspension Bridge Toll-house
(TL 537929)   'Toll Bar'
Littleport - Downham Market

About six miles south-west of Salter's Lode back up the New Bedford River, just inside the border with Cambridgeshire, there was at one time a toll-house at a place called Suspension Bridge.

The bridge in question took the Wisbech to Littleport road over the New River, and is shown on the early Ordnance Survey maps as 'Toll Bar', although its exact position is difficult to determine.

Salter's Lode Toll-house
(TF 586015)
Wisbech - Downham Market

photo: polystar

Very close to a complex waterway interchange at Salter's Lode Lock, there was until recently a small 'Telford' type toll-house controlling access to the river bank. The road here follows along parallel to the New Bedford River, also known as the Hundred Foot Drain.

The toll-house was built of the local Carstone with white brick dressings, a combination very common in Downham Market just two miles north-east. The brickwork here was particularly interesting with not only the quoins, but a drip mould detail carried out effectively. Unfortunately the toll-house has now been demolished to make way for a modern two storey house.

Fordham Toll-house
(TL 621989)   'T.P.'
Littleport - Downham Market

The road northwards from Littleport follows along the east bank of the river Great Ouse for some distance and further on it crosses the river Wissey just north of Hilgay. Here on the north bank just in the parish of Fordham, there was once a toll-house. It stood roughly where the road now the A10 by-passing Hilgay, rejoins its former route.

The Fordham tithe apportionment of 1840 showed it as 'Toll House and Garden' and owned by 'Turnpike Commissioners'.

Littleport Bridge Toll-house (Cambs)
TL 578877   'T.P.'
Mildenhall - Littleport etc

photo: polystar

The turnpike road north-westwards from Mildenhall in Suffolk continues in its flat Fenland manner for about nine miles, until it reaches the river Great Ouse at Littleport.

Here on the east bank just outside the town, there still stands the toll-house that controlled this particular trust's road. Now luckily by-passed because the road bridge has been moved downstream slightly, it can be seen to be similar to the toll-house at Lynn Road, Wisbech, but with an extra bay.

Brick built, it has a similar first floor recessed panel (now painted) for the toll-board and at least one useful small side window.

Wilton Bridge Toll-house
(TL 724868)   'T.G.'
Mildenhall - Littleport etc

North of Mildenhall, the northern end of the road through Lakenheath to Hockwold was controlled by a toll-house just inside the Norfolk border adjoining Wilton Bridge.

This now appears to have been lost and may have gone when the bridge was rebuilt: the current bridge is not the 'Suspension Bridge' shown on the first edition 1" Ordnance Survey maps just south of the designation 'T.G.'

Setchey Toll-house
TF 636136
Kings Lynn - Stoke Ferry etc.

photo: polystar

Another apparent example of a 'Telford' type toll-house can be found at Setchey, four miles south of Kings Lynn just north of the bridge over the River Nar.

Unlike its fenland neighbours, this one is on the greensand ridge and accordingly built of the local Carstone with white brick dressings. It has 'gothick' style windows and a door to match, with unusually a pantiled roof, complete with hipped joints, that are not easy to execute.

The North Runcton tithe records list two properties here as owned by 'Trustees of Turnpike': this one as 'Toll-House and Garden' and another just south of the river as 'Cottage', possibly an earlier toll-house.

Stoke Ferry Toll-house
(TL 707999)   'T.P.'
Stoke Ferry - Barton etc.

In the centre of the village of Stoke Ferry roads from Barton Bendish and Cockley Cley met the Thetford to Kings Lynn main road.

A building tight on the eastern side of the junction shown on early 25" maps, but now gone, was probably the toll-house. The Stoke Ferry tithe apportionment of 1841 shows only 'House and Garden' at this location, but owned by 'Trustees of Turnpike'.

Four Lost Kings Lynn Toll-houses

Kings Lynn - Hillington / Wisbech / Stoke Ferry

Gaywood Toll-house
(TF 639211)   'T.G.'
Kings Lynn - Hillington

North-west of Kings Lynn, the road to Hillington was controlled by a toll-house at Gaywood, now a suburb of the town.

Now lost, the toll-house was shown on the Gaywood tithe map of 1838 as 'Toll' and included in the apportionment as 'Toll House and Garden' owned by 'Turnpike Commissioners'.

Fairstead Toll-house
(TF 641204)   'T.P.'
Kings Lynn - Hillington

Half a mile south of the Gaywood toll-house and in the same parish, there was another at Fairstead, controlling the road eastwards to Gayton, the other branch of this trust's routes.

It was similarly shown on the tithe map as 'Toll Bar', and described in each column of the apportionment as 'do.' (i.e. ditto).

South Lynn Toll-house
(TF 619188)
Wisbech - South Lynn etc.

Now the site of the late Victorian South Lynn Baptist Church, this junction of roads from Wisbech and Wiggenhall at one time had its own toll-house.

The toll-house was shown on the Kings Lynn tithe apportionment of 1844 as 'Toll House and Garden' owned by 'South Lynn Commissioners', and was still there on the first edition 25" Ordnance Survey map of 1887.

Hardwick Toll-house
(TF 637179)   'Hardwick Toll'
Kings Lynn - Stoke Ferry etc.

About a mile nearer Kings Lynn than the North Runcton toll-house, the first edition 1" Ordnance Survey map also shows 'Hardwick Toll', at the foot of Constitution Hill.

The tithe map indicates a possible building at this location, but only shows 'Cottage and Garden' in the apportionment. This probably represents an earlier site for the control of this road, superseded by the North Runcton toll-house later in the 19th Century.

North Runcton Toll-house
TF 647165   'Toll'
Kings Lynn - Stoke Ferry etc.

photo: polystar

A branch of the Kings Lynn to Stoke Ferry turnpike trust's roads went eastwards to the villages of East Walton and Narborough. Access to this was controlled by a toll-house at North Runcton, three miles out of Kings Lynn.

Reminiscent of the Setchey toll-house, built of Carstone with white brick dressings and a hipped pantile roof, it is rectangular in plan and has pointed window heads.

It has survived by being by-passed, facing the old road with a new one at its rear. The North Runcton tithe records of 1841 list the building as 'Toll-House & Garden' owned by 'Trustees of Turnpike'.

Fincham Toll-house
(TF 682063)   'Toll'
Downham Market - Barton etc.

The road eastwards from Downham Market towards Swaffham appears to have had a gate at Fincham, where there remains no trace of a toll-house now. It was situated at a junction at the west end of the village.

The first edition 1" Ordnance Survey map is marked here with the word 'Toll', and the 1840 Fincham tithe apportionment lists 'Toll House' owned by 'Turnpike Trustees'.

Westgate Toll-house, Wells next the Sea
TF 913432
Wells - Fakenham etc.

photo: polystar

Whilst the roads around Kings Lynn nearly join up with those centred on Norwich near Swaffham, the only true link by turnpike road was via the roads of the Wells and Fakenham trust further north.

Known as 'Westgate Tollbar', this toll-house at the south-west edge of Wells next the Sea controlled the western route southwards towards Fakenham. The building sits diagonally across a sharp corner with good views down both approaches. Built of white brick with a slate roof, it may be contemporary with the railway that runs parallel behind the building, which would explain its 'railway architecture' appearance.

Wells next the Sea E Toll-house
(TF 922430)   'T.G.'
Wells - Fakenham etc.

Just south-east of Wells next the Sea, where the coast road to Sheringham splits from the road south to Walsingham, there was a further toll-house owned by this trust, controlling the eastern exit from Wells.

Situated in the fork of the road, it was probably removed for road improvements. It appeared on the tithe map of 1843, but like its companion pictured above, it was not shown on the first edition 1" Ordnance Survey.

Little Walsingham Toll-house
TF 940367   'T.G.'
Wells - Fakenham etc.

photo: polystar

Further south on the eastern route from Wells to Fakenham there is another surviving toll-house for this trust, just east of Little Walsingham.

With two storeys and built of brick with a hipped slate roof, it has an unusual first floor projecting window over an elaborate doorcase.

The first edition 1" Ordnance Survey has it as 'T.G.', whilst the 25" records 'Tollbar Plantation' to its rear.

Further south still, where both routes approach Fakenham, there are two more 'T.G.' sites (TF 905324 & 914319), but whether these had toll-houses is uncertain.

Sculthorpe Toll-house
(TF 913307)   'T.G.'
Wells - Fakenham etc.

North-west of Fakenham and now within the by-pass, the first edition 1" Ordnance Survey map shows a third site marked 'T.G.' within a mile of the two just mentioned.

This one did have a toll-house, which appeared on the Sculthorpe tithe map of 1838, described in the apportionment as 'Tollhouse and Garden' owned by 'Turnpike Road, Trustees of'. It also appeared on the Fakenham tithe map just outside the boundary as 'Toll Gate'.

41

Stone Cross Toll-house
TG 279283
Norwich - North Walsham

photo: polystar

This roadside bungalow just south of North Walsham is known as Monument Cottage, on account of the nearby medieval stone cross. It sits close to the highway edge and gives away its purpose with the small side windows in the gables for good views of approaching traffic.

We will see that this type of single storey toll-house with a simple pantile roof and gable parapet is fairly typical of the eastern parts of Norfolk as well as Suffolk.

The 1843 tithe apportionment lists it simply as 'Cottage and Garden', but the adjoining field is 'Old Tollgate Pightle', suggesting it was no longer used by then.

Horstead Toll-house
(TG 263194) 'T.G.'
Norwich - North Walsham

About seven miles south of Stone Cross, the North Walsham road had a further toll-house at Horstead.

The junction it guarded has now been by-passed by a short length of road straightening, however the building is long gone.

It too had appeared on the tithe map, the apportionment of 1841 listing it as 'Tollgate', owned by 'Turnpike Trustees'.

Westwick Toll-house
TG 279278   'T.G.'
Norwich - North Walsham

photo: polystar

One of a pair of hexagonal buildings that sit either side of the road about half a mile south of Monument Cottage, they appear not to be lodges as there are no driveways leading to them. They do however mark the northern boundary of Westwick parish, whose southern boundary is also marked by two larger lodges either side of the road about two miles further south.

The early Ordnance Survey maps show 'T.G.' at this point and both appear on the tithe map of 1844, so it seems that one of these was probably a replacement for Monument Cottage. The eastern one of the pair, shown above, retains the name 'Tollbar Cottage'.

Northrepps Toll-house
(TG 229391)   'T.G.'
Norwich - Aylsham etc.

About two miles south of Cromer at Crossdale Street in the parish of Northrepps stood the last in a series of toll-houses on the Norwich to Cromer road, most of which have now disappeared.

The Northrepps tithe map of 1840 showed it as 'Tollgate', whilst the apportionment described it as simply 'Cottage and Garden', but owned by 'Trustees for Norwich & Cromer Turnpike'.

Crostwick Toll-house
(TG 253152)   'T.G.'
Norwich - North Walsham

photo: ivy miller

Nearest Norwich on the North Walsham road, there was a toll-house at Crostwick, the site now nearly engulfed by the large village of Spixworth.

This photograph was kindly supplied by the owner of the bungalow, 'Toll-Bar Cottage', that now occupies the site and shows the toll-house appearing to be semi-detached. Apparently the business of toll collecting was undertaken in the lean to extension on the north side adjoining the cross-roads.

The tithe map of 1839 shows it as 'Toll Gate', the apportionment listing it as 'Cottage and Garden' owned by 'Trustees of Turnpike Road'.

Hanworth Toll-house
(TG 213357)   'T.G.'
Norwich - Aylsham etc.

About a mile south of the village of Roughton, on the Norwich to Cromer road, there was at one time a toll-house at a junction with a lane leading off eastwards to Thorpe Market.

The Hanworth tithe apportionment of 1840 lists the field adjoining the building shown on the map to the north-east side of the junction as 'Tollgate Pightle'. By 1906 the second edition 25" OS map shows no trace of the building.

Marsham Toll-house
TG 198246
Norwich - Aylsham etc.

photo: polystar

Now extended to the south, even the original portion of the toll-house at Marsham seems unduly large compared to others of the single storey brick and pantile type. It has a gable window to the south and presumably one of the five front windows was originally the door.

This toll-house replaced an earlier one shown as 'T.G.' at TG 198243 on the early 1" Ordnance Survey map. The original toll-house, roughly opposite the end of Fengate Lane, was demolished to form a new driveway to Bolwick Hall. Subsequently the main road has been moved westwards a short distance, leaving the toll-house safely by-passed in wooded seclusion.

Erpingham Toll-house
(TG 199308) 'T.G.'
Norwich - Aylsham etc.

The Norwich to Cromer main road originally left Aylsham on a more westerly route than at present. To the south of the village of Erpingham there was a toll-house at a cross-roads, now long gone.

The building was shown on the 1885 first edition 25" OS map and was listed as 'House and Gate' on the tithe apportionment of 1840, owned by 'Trustees of Cromer Turnpike'.

Five More Lost Toll-houses

Norwich - Aylsham

Blickling Toll-house
(TG 191290)   'T.G.'
Norwich - Aylsham etc.

Just south of the village of Ingworth on the old route north of Aylsham, there was a toll-house at a road junction leading off towards Blickling Hall.

Like the Hanworth example it had gone by 1906, but had made an earlier appearance in the records. The Blickling tithe apportionment of 1841 lists it as 'Toll Bar House and Garden', although in the ownership of the Dowager Lady Caroline Suffield.

Hellesdon N Toll-house
(TG 215124)   'T.G.'
Norwich - Aylsham etc.

Before the building of Norwich Airport, there was a fork at Hellesdon, where the Holt and Aylsham roads separated. Here there was a toll-house, guarding this approach to Norwich.

It was shown as 'Turnpike' on the tithe map of 1839, but the area has long since been redeveloped as Norwich has grown out around it.

Norwich - Fakenham

Langor Bridge Toll-house
(TF 962292)   'T.G.'
Norwich - Fakenham

About three miles south-east of Fakenham the first edition 1" Ordnance Survey map shows another 'T.G.' at Langor Bridge, but like those the other side of Fakenham nothing remains.

The toll-house here controlled the far end of the Norwich to Fakenham trust's route and was just to the east of a bridge over both a river and the Lynn and Fakenham Railway.

Hellesdon Toll-houses
(TG 201118 + 199113)   'T.G.'
Norwich - Fakenham

The Norwich end of this same road was served by a toll-house on the north side of a cross-roads in Hellesdon, which was probably demolished for road widening. Opposite the site a Victorian hospital lodge mirrors the toll-house idea with a small octagonal wing.

About half a mile south-west there was a further toll-house known as Hellesdon Lower Gate, now replaced by a modern bungalow.

Bawdeswell Toll-house
TG 049208   'T.G.'
Norwich - Fakenham

photo: polystar

Standing at the east end of the village of Bawdeswell, this well presented toll-house guards the outer end of the Norwich to Fakenham road, now the A1067. Recently refurbished with original detailing to its door and windows, this is probably a result of its being listed grade II.

It is a single storey bungalow type, of brick construction with a hipped pantile roof, markedly different to the 'Telford' type of single storey toll-house we have seen in the west of the county.

The tithe map apportionment of 1845 described it as 'Cottage and Garden' owned by 'Turnpike, Trustees of'.

Swaffham Toll-house
(TF 845095)   'T.P.'
Norwich - Swaffham etc.

The western end of the Norwich to Swaffham road was controlled by a toll-house about a mile east of Swaffham. It was on the north-west corner of the cross-roads with the Peddars Way, now a little to the south of the re-aligned main A47.

It had been listed as 'Toll Bar House Gardens etc.' in the 1843 Swaffham tithe apportionment, and was owned by 'Swaffham Turnpike, the Trustees for'.

Wendling 'Old Toll House'
TF 926129
Norwich - Swaffham etc.

photo: polystar

This small flint and brick bungalow known as 'The Old Toll House' certainly looks the part, not dissimilar in form to the other slightly doubtful toll-house we saw at Outwell.

Like that one, there is no record of a toll-house here on old maps or turnpike records seen thus far.

However it is on a turnpike road and its small bay to the west would enable control of a lane joining the main road from the north, now truncated by the by-pass.

East Dereham Toll-house
(TF 982133)   'T.G.'
Norwich - Swaffham etc.

The western approaches to East Dereham were controlled by a toll-house at a junction just west of the town.

Like the Etling Green toll-house to the east, the site has now been by-passed, but unfortunately this example has not survived.

This one did appear on the first edition 1" Ordnance Survey but has not been located on tithe records.

Etling Green Toll-house
TG 016139
Norwich - Swaffham etc.

photo: polystar

Just east of East Dereham, there is a toll-house at Etling Green, now by-passed by the A47 trunk road.

Another of the single storey pantile type, it is known as 'Tollgate Cottage. Although now safe from the road, it has had the central doorway blocked up and been subjected to an application of not very realistic false timbering.

East Dereham's tithe apportionment of 1840 lists it as 'Cottage and Garden' owned by 'Turnpike Trustees', but for some reason it does not appear on the early 1" OS maps. Its purpose is confirmed by its general form, proximity to the road and the small side windows.

Scoulton Toll-house
(TG 000015)
Norwich - Watton

The Norwich to Watton turnpike road had two toll-houses, both now demolished. At the Watton end the 1906 second edition 25" OS map shows a likely building on the parish boundary between Scoulton and Hingham.

The purpose is remembered in the nearby 'Tollgate Farm', where a remnant of a toll-board was found (see p.21). Although the tithe map is incomplete here, the 1839 apportionment lists 'Part Tollgate House & Garden' in the ownership of 'Turnpike, Trustees for the'.

East Tuddenham Toll-house
TG 069112   'T.G.'
Norwich - Swaffham etc.

photo: polystar

This red brick and pantile house, known as 'Tollgate Farm', adjoining East Tuddenham's parish boundary, controlled a branch of the Norwich to Swaffham turnpike serving Mattishall and Yaxham, as confirmed by the nearby milestone.

Unlike many Tollgate Farms, this one is actually the old toll-house, albeit much extended at the rear. This is borne out by the small side window hidden behind the fence to the west of the house. It is also fairly near the edge of the highway and compares favourably with the toll-house at Earlham shown opposite.

The 1839 tithe apportionment lists it as 'Toll Gate House etc.' owned by 'Trustees for Mattishall Turnpike'.

Colney Toll-house
(TG 186082)   'T.G.'
Norwich - Watton

At the Norwich end of the Watton road there was a toll-house in the village of Colney, now at the edge of greater Norwich.

It appeared as 'T.G.' on the first edition 1" Ordnance Survey map and was described in the 1840 tithe apportionment as 'House and Garden' owned by 'Turnpike Trustees'.

Earlham Toll-house
TG 192097
Norwich - Swaffham etc.

photo: polystar

Absorbed within greater Norwich's suburb of New Costessey, this toll-house is now semi-detached, but retains enough of its original form to be recognisable for what it is.

The blanked out first floor window may be either for a toll-board, or a result of its semi-detachment, when the party wall was inserted. Presumably it also had a central doorway and left hand window at one time, both now blocked up because of the nearby busy road.

Shown on the tithe map for Earlham St Mary of 1846 as 'Toll Gate', it was listed in the apportionment as 'Toll Gate House' owned by 'Trustees of the Dereham Turnpike'.

Kilverstone Toll-house
(TL 891851)   'T.G.'
Norwich - Thetford

The Thetford end of this road from Norwich had a toll-house, about two miles out of the town, near Kilverstone Hall.

Sited near the roundabout where the dual carriageway by-pass now leaves the original route to loop around the north of Thetford, the toll-house appears to have been lost during the road improvements.

This may be a later toll-house as no trace of it can be found in the tithe records.

Cringleford Toll-house
TG 200059   'T.G.'
Norwich - Thetford

photo: polystar

The Hethersett to Attleborough road was the earliest turnpike road in Norfolk. It was extended by later acts to become the Norwich to Thetford road, now the A11.

The Norwich end of this was controlled by the toll-house at Cringleford about three miles from the city centre. The original doorway onto the road is now blocked as are any ground floor windows there may have been; the house has been re-orientated to face its side garden.

It appeared on the 1842 tithe map apportionment as 'Cottage and Toll House' owned by 'Trustees of the Turnpike Road'.

Bunwell Toll-house
(TM 137933)   'T.G.'
Norwich - New Buckenham

The outer end of the Norwich to New Buckenham trust's road had a toll-house at Bunwell, recorded in the 1839 tithe apportionment as 'Cottage and Garden' owned by 'Turnpike Trustees'.

It was on the east side of the road and opposite the 1885 first edition 25" Ordnance Survey map showed 'Tollgate Farm'.

Litcham Toll-house
TF 888178
Not a Turnpike Road

photo: polystar

Between Gayton, 7 miles east of Kings Lynn, and Bawdeswell, on the Norwich to Fakenham road, there lie about twenty miles. Here the line of the present B1145 provided an alternative and convenient route through central western Norfolk, avoiding the need to pay tolls at Swaffham, East Dereham or Fakenham.

This house called Fourways' is at the eastern end of the village of Litcham and is reputedly a toll-house that collected money from travellers from the east. Those from the west paid at the Bull Inn in the village. It is not clear who collected the tolls, but apparently they stopped in 1912.

Thelveton Toll-house
(TM 161807) 'T.G.'
Norwich - Scole Bridge

About two miles short of the Suffolk border, the Norwich to Scole road had its final toll-house at Thelveton.

Although now by-passed by the Dickleburgh relief road, nothing remains except the memory preserved in the nearby Tollgate Farm, and the words 'Tollgate House' on the old 25" Ordnance Survey map.

Costessey Toll-house
TG 182130   'Toll bar'
Private Road

photo: polystar

Although not on a turnpike road, there is clearly a 'Toll bar', which had this attendant toll-house, marked on the first edition 1" OS map at this location. Now known as Bridge Cottage, it sits in glorious isolation beside the River Wensum adjoining the position of a former bridge removed in the 1970's.

The trackway here was privately owned by John Culley, the miller from Costessey, also one of the Dereham Turnpike trustees. He apparently charged his own tolls for use of the track, presumably a convenient shortcut between the villages of Drayton and Costessey, north and south of the river respectively.

Saxlingham Toll-houses
(TM 212979)   'T.G.'
Norwich - Scole Bridge

Known as Newton Gate, but actually just over the River Tas in the parish of Saxlingham, there was a toll-house about midway along the Norwich to Scole route. The old bridge remains next to the new road and the new bridge is roughly where the toll-house once stood.

It was described as 'Toll House and Garden', owned by 'Trustees of the London Turnpike Road' in the tithe apportionment of 1842, along with a second identical entry for another about a quarter mile to the south, controlling a side lane to Foxhole (TM 212976).

Filby Heath Toll-house
TG 501129   'T.G.'
Norwich - Caister Causeway

photo: polystar

Whilst the roads south of Norwich appear to have left us little to look at, those eastwards do have the toll-house at Filby Heath near Caister, at the eastern end of the original Norwich to Great Yarmouth road.

Here we find another of our bungalow type toll-houses. This one has been re-roofed with modern tiles and the smaller window is probably where the doorway was.

Now safely by-passed, it remains very close to the highway edge. It was listed in the tithe apportionment of 1841 as 'Tollhouse and Garden' owned by 'Trustees of Roads'.

Keswick Toll-houses
(TG 219049)   2x'T.G.'
Norwich - Scole Bridge

The inner end of the New Buckenham road joined the Norwich to Scole road at Harford Bridge in the parish of Keswick, now just on the southern edge of Norwich.

Here there were two toll-houses, one controlling each route. Both were listed in the 1847 tithe apportionment as 'House and Garden' owned by 'Turnpike, Trustees of''.

Bure Bridge Toll-houses, Great Yarmouth
(TG 521080)
Great Yarmouth - Acle etc.

photo: peter allard

The original route from Norwich to Great Yarmouth via Caister was in 1831 replaced by a new road across the marshes, now known as the 'Acle Straight'.

The far eastern end of this new road was at first controlled by a toll-house in Great Yarmouth on the eastern bank of the river adjoining the 'Suspension Bridge' over the River Bure.

This original building actually lasted until 1951, but its use as a toll-house was soon superseded in 1837 by another, as shown above, on the more level western bank, where traffic could stop more easily to pay the tolls.

Thorpe St Andrew Toll-houses
(TG 250083 & 281087)   'T.G.'
Norwich - Caister Causeway

The Norwich end of the Great Yarmouth road was controlled by one or more toll-houses at Thorpe St. Andrew.

The first edition 1" Ordnance Survey map shows 'T.G.' about three miles from the city centre and not very far from where there remains a good cast iron milestone. However the tithe apportionment of 1842 for Thorpe indicates the site nearer the city centre: 'Toll house and Garden' owned by 'Norwich and Yarmouth Turnpike, Trustees of'.

Vauxhall Toll-house, Great Yarmouth
(TG 518083)
Great Yarmouth - Acle etc.

photo: peter allard

Both the Runham and the western Bure Bridge toll-houses were made redundant in 1852 by the new toll-house built near Vauxhall station to prevent the evasion of tolls, which had become a problem since the railway bridge was built in 1848.

Octagonal and built of brick with a slate roof, this single storey toll-house was not unlike the one at Botesdale in Suffolk.

In their turn, the Vauxhall and both Bure Bridge toll-houses, along with the Bowspring bridge of 1847 (that had replaced the earlier Suspension bridge) were all demolished in the early 1950's to make way for the present girder bridge.

> **Runham Toll-house**
> (TG 515089)   'T.G.'
> *Great Yarmouth - Acle etc.*
>
> The eastern end of the Acle Straight was controlled by a toll-house on the south side of the bend at Runham.
>
> Out of town, relative to the Bure Bridge toll-houses, this controlled access to the main road from several side lanes that joined the route here. It was made redundant by the 1852 Vauxhall toll-house, but parts of it are believed to have survived as Strawberry Farm up until the 1960's.

Five Lost Broadland Toll-houses

Great Yarmouth - Acle etc Ipswich - South Town

Acle Toll-house
(TG 423096)   'T.G.'
Great Yarmouth - Acle etc.

The main western approach to the Acle Straight was controlled by a toll-house at Acle itself, albeit a little out of the village.

It appeared on the 1838 tithe map as 'Toll Gate' and was listed in the 1840 tithe apportionment as 'Toll House', owned by 'Acle and Yarmouth Turnpike Trustees'.

Gorleston Toll-house
(TG 520018)
Ipswich - South Town

The final northern stretch of the Ipswich to South Town road had two toll-houses between Lowestoft and Great Yarmouth, both now lost.

The northern one was on the southern outskirts of Gorleston.

It appeared on the first edition 25" Ordnance Survey map of 1885 (sheet 2/15) as 'Old Toll House'.

Halvergate Toll-houses
(TG 428069)   'T.G.'
Great Yarmouth - Acle etc.

A subsidiary approach to the western end of Acle Straight was possible via Halvergate, so that a further toll-house was needed there, just east of the village.

This was listed in the 1842 Halvergate tithe apportionment as 'Cottage—Turnpike Gate', owned by 'Trustees of Turnpike'.

Where the two roads joined at Stracey Arms (TG 438090) a further 'Toll House' appeared on the tithe map, which judging by the local name 'Wooden Hut Corner', was something of a temporary structure.

Hopton Toll-house
(TG 525001)
Ipswich - South Town

About a mile south of the Gorleston toll-house, there was another at Hopton, on a site now by-passed by the modern road.

This stood roughly midway between Great Yarmouth and Lowestoft, and is also now demolished. Both of these toll-houses were originally in Suffolk, but their sites are now part of Norfolk.

It too appeared on the first edition 25" Ordnance Survey map (sheet 4/3) as 'Old Toll House'.

Haddiscoe Toll-house
TM 447970   'T.G.'
Little Yarmouth - Blythburgh

photo: polystar

The A145 road off the A12 northwards from Blythburgh was originally part of the Little Yarmouth turnpike, providing an alternative inland route northwards from Suffolk to Great Yarmouth.

Mainly within Suffolk, it passes through a section of Norfolk between Gillingham and Haddiscoe, where there is a relatively well preserved toll-house with its giveaway side windows and a large new window where the near central collector's doorway had been.

It appeared in Turnpike Trust minutes of April 1796: 'order placed for construction of turnpike and toll house, for sum of £98, at south end of Haddiscoe Dam'.

Gillingham Toll-house
(TM 412917)   'T.G.'
Little Yarmouth - Blythburgh

Where the Little Yarmouth route crossed over the Waveney into Beccles, there was a toll-house also described in the minutes of April 1796 as being at the north end of Gillingham Dam, the dam being the causeway upon which the road was constructed over the river's flood plain marshes.

Probably similar to the Haddiscoe one, it appeared in the tithe apportionment as 'Toll House & Garden', owned by 'Beccles Turnpike, Trustees of".

Great Yarmouth Toll House
TG 524072

And so to finish we come to Great Yarmouth in the far east of the county. Here we have the final toll-house, but not one as we have come to know them.

This old picture postcard depicting 'Old Toll House, Gt Yarmouth' shows the former Town Hall/ Market House there, a different kind of building altogether.

This is one of the type of building known in Scotland as a Tolbooth or Town-house, where market traders paid their dues and which also contained courts and a prison. It now serves as a museum.

> ### South Town Toll-house
> (TG 523064)
> *South Town*
>
> The final mile of the Ipswich to Great Yarmouth route was controlled by a separate trust from South Town into the centre of Great Yarmouth.
>
> This had its own toll-house at South Town, on the south-western bank of the river, but nothing can be found of it today.

5.0 Appendix: The Impostors

Buildings in Norfolk that are not Toll-houses

When researching and looking for toll-houses in any county, one's first attempts will undoubtedly focus on various octagonal ended buildings near the roadside that seem to offer themselves up as likely candidates.

We have seen from the foregoing gazetteer that in Norfolk this type of toll-house, as found at Wiggenhall or Vauxhall, is certainly not the norm. In fact the norm for the area appears to be the foursquare two storey house or single storey bungalow, usually with a central porch and the requisite side gable windows for vision up and down the road, such as those found at East Tuddenham, Earlham, Marsham or Haddiscoe.

In order to prevent the inevitable "but what about the toll-house at ....?" type questions that might follow the publication of this book, the following appendix includes a fair selection of octagonal ended buildings from around the county. It seems that many such buildings were built, mainly as lodges or cottages ornées. Thus the octagonal form is certainly not unknown in Norfolk as the following pages will testify, it is just that the toll-house builders chose not to use it for some reason.

These 'impostors' are presented in roughly the same order as the main gazetteer of toll-houses, i.e. from west to east across the county. Many of these are from parishes where a toll-house was expected to be found, and some of them have for varying lengths of time led the author slightly astray. It is hoped that diligent research has by now weeded out all such impostors from the gazetteer proper, so that they are all relegated to this appendix.

The author will of course be pleased to hear enquiries of the form "but what about the impostor at ....?", they almost warrant a book of their own!

Hat & Feather, Lords Bridge
TF 572123

This foursquare building with a blanked out window at first floor level and blocked in doorway is not unlike the Wisbech or Littleport toll-houses from further across the Fens.

Just the other side of the Smeeth Lode Mill Basin opposite the real Lord's Bridge toll-house on the cross-roads, diligent mapwork has shown that this was in fact a former Public House, shown on the 1905 1st edition 25" OS map as the 'Hat and Feather'.

photo: polystar

Round House, Hanworth
TG 211339

In between the Erpingham and Hanworth toll-houses, which were only three miles apart on the Norwich to Cromer road, this building would have been superfluous as a toll-house.

It is constructed of flint with white brick dressings, and although it looks the part it is not a toll-house.

The tithe apportionment for Hanworth of 1840 has the site occupied by 'House, School Buildings and Garden'. More recently the building has been a Post Office.

photo: polystar

Lodge at Felbrigg
TG 204401

About two miles south of Cromer at TG 204401 but not on the turnpike route, the red brick octagonal lodge shown below would pass as a tollhouse elsewhere in the country.

It is however a simple estate lodge, with an extra wing to one side making up for the limited space in the octagonal two storey part. Part of the Felbrigg House estate, it was probably a gamekeeper's cottage.

Another small building, called Wood Lodge, with the presence of a tollhouse, looking directly down a long straight stretch of what was the Norwich to North Walsham turnpike road is shown opposite above.

Built in red brick with a pyramidal hipped slate roof and 'gothick' pointed windows, it looks promising, but is simply another lodge to the Westwick Estate (see p.43).

A little to the south of Wood Lodge, there is another called Park Lodge on the other side of the road, guarding yet another entrance to the Westwick Estate.

This one is L-shaped in plan with a protruding octagonal bay on the corner giving good all round vision. Like Wood Lodge, it is built of red brick with a slate roof, but this time has a more classical look with its rubbed brick flat window heads.

photo: polystar

Wood Lodge and Park Lodge, Westwick
TG 277273 & TG 279268

photo: polystar

photo: polystar

65

Octagonal Bays, Market Square, Reepham
TG 100228

The small town of Reepham, north-west of Norwich, has in one corner of its Market Place a former coaching inn, the Kings Arms. The eastern cross-wing of this projects as a normal gable, whilst the western one is formed into a toll-house like octagonal bay with a steep plaintile roof.

To top this a property two doors further west has a more recent octagonal bay on its frontage, slate roofed above decorative tilehanging and containing a Victorian shopfront.

Two for the price of one, but neither is a toll-house.

photo: polystar

Rose Cottage, Litcham
TF 882181

This small single storey cottage, just north of Litcham village, itself not on a turnpike road (see p.53), is not of much use for any form of toll collecting. It sits in the fork of two very minor lanes leading nowhere in particular.

However with its 'gothick' pointed window heads and projecting octagonal bay with central doorway, it does have something of the character of one of the 'Telford' type toll-houses from the Fens.

photo: polystar

Alms Cottage, Brisley
TF 950215

Situated opposite Brisley church on the outside of a bend in the road going around the churchyard, this building, like many a toll-house is well placed to see both ways along the road.

It certainly looks the part with its hipped slate roof around octagonal ended walls with 'gothick' windows in white brick surrounds. However it is grade II listed and was formerly three almshouses, now all one dwelling.

Not on a turnpike road, it is nevertheless on the old coaching route that ran through west Norfolk via Litcham (see p.53).

photo: polystar

Beehive Lodge, Costessey
TG 148124

Most definitely a building of the turnpike era and looking the part with its 'gothick' windows, this building is not a toll-house. It has a circular thatched roof, white painted brick walls and rustic columns.

It is in fact a grade II listed lodge to Costessey Hall, situated in Ringland Lane, which follows the south bank of the River Wensum west of Costessey village.

This route is far too tortuous, and possibly treacherous so near the river in places, to have served as a turnpike road.

photo: polystar

Round House, Dereham Road, Costessey
TG 169103

This unusual octagonal house of white painted brick with a pantile roof is just off the old A47 about a mile and a half west of the Earlham toll-house.

It is grade II listed and described in the listing as a former toll-house, supposedly marked as such on the 1840 tithe map.

Unfortunately the map has no such text on it and the apportionment simply describes a 'Cottage and Gardens' owned by Lord Stafford of Costessey Hall.

photo: polystar

The Gatehouse, Norwich
TG 205095

A roundhouse of sorts, this wing of the Gatehouse public house is strategically positioned where a minor road off the old A47 towards East Dereham and Swaffham branches off to the north.

Although the pub was built in 1934, the name is suggestive, as is the nearby Tollhouse Road. These names may of course refer to St Benedict's Gate in the old city walls a mile and a half to the east, where tolls were reputedly collected, or the Earlham toll-house three quarters of a mile further west.

The Earlham tithe map of 1846 simply shows a meadow here.

photo: polystar

Lodge, Roudham
TL 957872

This small octagonal cottage with an octagonal extension near the village of Bridgham, north-east of Thetford, has recently been renovated.

In a very picturesque setting near the ruins of Roudham Church, it was built as a lodge adjoining a driveway to Roudham Hall. However, it stands about half a mile away from the Norwich to Thetford road and so could not have functioned as a toll-house.

Very much in the cottage ornée tradition it is rendered with 'gothick' windows and has an overhanging thatched roof carried on rustic timber columns.

photo: polystar

Roundhouse, Cringleford
TG 188056

Well positioned on Newmarket Road, this octagonal house is about a mile west of the actual Cringleford toll-house, serving the Norwich to Thetford trust.

Brick built with 'gothick' windows and a black pantile hipped roof, it certainly looks the part, although it is perhaps a little on the large side for a toll-house.

Grade II listed it is believed to have been constructed in 1805 as part of the Kerrison estate.

photo: polystar

Octagon House, Brooke
TG 295001

This unusual octagonal house is just outside the village of Brooke, south-east of Norwich. The Bungay road passes through the other end of the village and the Beccles road passes two miles to the north-east, but neither of these were turnpike roads.

Very similar to the Cringleford example we have just seen, it also has 'gothick' style pointed windows, but again is a little too large for a toll-house. The connection seems to be that it was also built for Sir Roger Kerrison, this time following the enclosures of 1801 to form the Brooke House estate.

photo: marion folkes

6.0 Bibliography

Albert, W. 1972 *Turnpike Road System in England 1663-1840* Cambridge

Alderton, D. & Booker, J. 1980 *The Industrial Archaeology of East Anglia* Batsford

Allard, P. 1997 *The Bure Bridge and Acle New Road Tollhouses* Yarmouth Archaeology

Chatwin, C.P. 1961 *East Anglia and Adjoining Areas* British Regional Geology HMSO

Clifford, S. & King, A. (eds) 1993 *Local Distinctiveness* Common Ground

Cossons, A. 1951 *The Turnpike Roads of Norfolk* Norfolk and Norwich Archaeological Society vol.XXX part III

Cruickshank, D. & Wyld, P. 1975 *London: The Art of Georgian Building* Architectural Press

Haines, C. 2000 *Marking The Miles A History of English Milestones* Haines

Harris, R. (ed) (no date) *Weald & Downland Open Air Museum Guidebook*

Mogg, E. 1829 *Paterson's Roads* London

Mowl, T. & Earnshaw, B. 1985 *Trumpet at a Distant Gate* Waterstone

Pawson, E. 1977 *Transport and Economy: The Turnpike Roads of Eighteenth Century Britain* Academic Press

Robinson, B. & Rose E. J. 2008 *Roads and Tracks* Poppyland

Searle, M. 1930 *Turnpikes and Toll-Bars* Hutchinson

Serjeant, W.R. & Penrose, D.G. (eds) 1973 *Suffolk Turnpikes* E Suffolk RO

Smith, P. 1970 *The Turnpike Age* Luton Museum and Art Gallery

Wade-Martins, P. (ed) 1994 *An Historical Atlas of Norfolk* Norfolk Museums

Wright, G.N. 1992 *Turnpike Roads* Shire

Of Related Interest:

The Toll-houses of Cornwall
Patrick Taylor   2001   £7.95
ISBN 0 902660 29 2   iv+80pp
Federation of Old Cornwall Societies

Companion volume to the present one, contains a similar introductory essay and history of the turnpike roads in Cornwall, followed by an extensive gazetteer of toll-houses and their former sites.

"A useful detailed county study with photographs of high quality" *Industrial Archaeology Review*

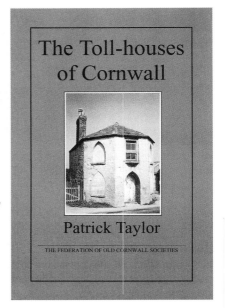

The Toll-houses of Suffolk
Patrick Taylor   2009   £7.95
ISBN 978 1 907154 00 3   iv+84pp
Polystar Press

The second volume based on the author's dissertation research, now part of a series.

Essentially the same format as this Norfolk volume: history of the turnpike roads, detailed gazetteer of the county plus an appendix on the impostors.

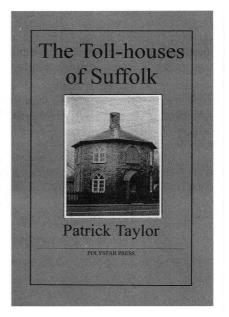